Knock on the Door

Knock on the Door

A Food Journal

SANDRA ANANI

StoryTerrace

Text Sandra Anani

Copyright © Sandra Anani

Text is private and confidential

First print May 2023

StoryTerrace

www.StoryTerrace.com

CONTENTS

INTRODUCTION   7

AUTUMN   11

  SALADS AND SOUPS
    Kale, Broccoli and Chickpea Salad   12
    Warm Broccoli Noodle Salad   13
    Freekeh Soup   14

  DIPS AND SIDES
    Pečene Paprike (Roasted Peppers)   15

  MAINS
    Mujaddara (Rice with Lentils)   16
    Creamy Mushroom Pasta Bake   17
    Saloni's Spinach and Paneer   18
    Spinach Fatayer   19

  DESSERT, SWEET TREATS AND BAKING
    Bajadere   21
    Giant Chunky Chocolate Chip Cookies   22

WINTER   25

  SALADS AND SOUPS
    Cabbage Salad   26
    Addas (Lentil Soup)   27
    Vegetable Soup   28
    Soup Noodles and Dumplings   29

  MAINS
    Aubergine Fatteh   30
    Maaloubeh   31
    Vojnički Pasulj (Army Beans)   32
    Macedonian Pie   33

  DESSERT, SWEET TREATS AND BAKING
    Strawberry and Chocolate Cake   35
    Brown Soda Bread   36

  DRINK
    Healthy Metabolism Activating Lemon Ginger Tonic Tea   37

SPRING 41

SALADS AND SOUPS
Fattoush — 42

DIPS AND SIDES
Tahini Dip — 43

MAINS
Italian Aubergine Bake (Parmigiana) — 44
Broadbean Maaloubeh — 45
Yoghurt Pasta — 46
Ful Mudammas — 47

DESSERT, SWEET TREATS AND BAKING
Cheese Board — 48
Koch (Semolina Sponge Cake) — 49
Raspberry Sherry Trifle — 50

DRINK
Turkish Coffee — 52

SUMMER 55

SALADS AND SOUPS
Tabbouleh — 56
Yogurt Cucumber Salad — 57

DIPS AND SIDES
Moutabal (Smoky Aubergine Dip) — 58

MAINS
Veggie Dream Stuffed Aubergines — 59
Greek Zucchini Spaghetti — 61
Mini Pizzas — 62

DESSERT, SWEET TREATS AND BAKING
Alyza's Waffles — 63
Lazy No-Bake Chocolate Cake — 64
Luqaimat — 65

DRINK
Mint Lemonade Mocktail — 66

TIPS FOR SUSTAINABLE LIVING 69

INTRODUCTION

My hope is for this book to take the reader on a journey, a brisk gastronomic tour through my life. I wish for you to experience its flavours, fragrances and emotions, and to return home safe, sound and maybe even a little inspired.

The best place to start to explain my interest in cooking is, perhaps unsurprisingly, the beginning. I travelled extensively as a child and grew up between Kuwait, Jordan, Croatia and Serbia, in a multi-cultural household where East met West and rules and social norms were blurred. I did not know then what a privilege this mixed background would turn out to be, but the luxury of growing up surrounded by a variety of cultures expanded both my worldview and my palate.

My mother has always been a no-nonsense cook. Her preference lay with simple, clean cuisine; the kind that is entirely undemanding, yet completely satisfying. I mostly remember her cooking steaks, escalopes or pommes frites in shallow pans of hot oil and whipping up giant bowls of delicious, crunchy salads, in hues of vibrant green or sensational red. But there was never anything which required her to stand in front of the stove stirring for hours. This logic also extended to desserts, and her speciality was simple, no-bake cakes made up of layers of creamy custard and biscuits. I was always thrilled to see them when I opened the fridge!

My father was a great lover of food, and therefore it played a key role in our lives. We were always eating out, trying new places, off on hurried trips in the car to the latest new kiosk offering tasty, searing hot bites. I had no concept of this being uncommon; I was a child, with little to compare my home life to. Doesn't everyone regularly eat roast beef sandwiches from Hardee's for supper?

Another mainstay of my childhood were yearly trips to visit my grandmother. We would return home to Kuwait and all my friends and their mothers would comment on how pudgy I had become. The main culprit for this was the trove of treats my grandmother kept stashed in a corner of her kitchen for me; heaps of sparkly, crinkly packets, both savoury and sweet. I did not understand it at the time, but I now look back fondly on the effort, consideration and thought she put into making me feel loved and welcome, and realise how much she wanted to spoil me.

Growing up around all of this I developed a love of food, obviously, but I had not yet connected it to cooking. I recall, when my family went to dine in fine restaurants and bijou cafes as a child,

Introduction

gazing up at huge gorgeous cakes through display cases blurred with condensation, admiring the piped swirls of whipped cream and glistening glacé cherries. It all felt like magic to me; I had no concept of how such a thing might come to be.

Trying to pinpoint when exactly I started to make that connection between food and cooking is tricky, but I imagine a shift began around the time I was old enough for school, began making friends and visiting them at their homes. I developed some awareness of how atypical my household had been and started observing how other people's families did things; how my friends' Middle Eastern mothers would spend hours in the kitchen, painstakingly preparing beautifully elaborate dishes, and the amount of work that went into every single meal they served.

The shift was somewhat gradual, but one moment does stand out. I was probably around twelve years old, visiting one of my school friends, when she suggested we make a pizza. That simple question completely blew me away; I had never thought of pizza as something anyone could make at home, let alone us kids! After I got over my initial shock, we did indeed make a pizza that day, as well as a huge mess I'm sure, but the seed had been planted.

It was around the age of twelve that I also started my life as a vegetarian. This has deeply influenced my life, and this book too, as it is full of vegan and vegetarian recipes for you to enjoy.

My mother noticed my budding interest in cooking and encouraged me, buying me lots of cookbooks which I would read cover to cover. It was soon time to put my freshly acquired knowledge to the test, to . . . mixed results. There were clouds of flour, burnt food, half-baked cakes, and other minor kitchen disasters, but no one told me to stop, and so I carried on. Even when things were not going my way, I remember thoroughly enjoying the experience, and looking back I was learning valuable lessons that would serve me far beyond the kitchen: you won't always be successful from the start, nor will you succeed every time; sometimes things don't quite work out, even if you follow each step exactly.

I kept trying for a few years, developing my skills, and eventually I must have become quite good because people started to ask me to make cakes for their parties! I was a university student by then, and thrilled at the opportunity to make some spending money. If we had access to things like social media at the time, I might have wanted to market myself and pursue that career path further, but it was the '90s, so word of mouth had to do. Even so, my little side business got pretty popular. All of this practise allowed me to hone my baking skills, and I still have and use many recipes from this period of my life, a few of which I have included here.

I have carried on learning ever since, discovering new dishes through work, travel, necessity and most importantly through all of the people I have met who were generous enough to share their knowledge with me.

To this day I love to cook, not just for the end result but for the process of it; from gathering ingredients and inspiration, to setting the perfect ambience and even the mistakes that inevitably occur along the way. We all must feed ourselves somehow, and so I try to appreciate the small things that help me find beauty in what could otherwise be a chore, like finding the first good

Introduction

tomatoes of the summer, or pouring myself a glass of red wine and playing Pavarotti in the background while I prepare a pasta dish.

But the true joy of food is, to me, felt most in those moments when we share it with others. It is with this in mind I named this book A Knock at the Door, after the sound that heralds the start of every social engagement, a promise of smiling faces and kisses on the cheek. It takes me back all the way to my childhood, when it reliably meant either friends or family visiting, bringing with them flowers, chocolates, cakes, and other delicacies.

I firmly believe there is no better way to catch up and connect with people than over a meal, and that nothing makes me feel as known and cared for as someone preparing a special dish for me. So I hope this book will be a celebration of the ones I love, and everything they have given me.

I also take inspiration from Victorian values; there is no food waste in my kitchen, everything is needed and has a use. I have always considered sustainability in my life, how much influence I have as an individual and the impact I have on my environment and community.

I have therefore structured this book to follow the seasons, using seasonally available produce and inspiration, and included menu planning sheets to help reduce waste, as well as some sustainability tips. The recipes are all global, delicious and vegetarian. I hope you enjoy them!

> *I would like to bring to the attention of the reader that there's a mixture of measurements in the ingredients lists, which is due to the fact that the recipes were collected at different times, from different people and from different geographic locations. As I didn't want to compromise the recipes or dilute the authenticity, I kept the measurements as they were given to me.*

AUTUMN

Salads and Soups

KALE, BROCCOLI AND CHICKPEA SALAD

This recipe stems from my desire to have quick but healthy meals. In a pinch, you can replace the broccoli with cauliflower florets or chopped spinach.

For the dressing:

2 tablespoons olive oil
2 tablespoons white wine vinegar

1 clove garlic, minced
1 tablespoon chopped parsley

For the salad:

1 large bowlful kale, washed and chopped
1 can chickpeas, drained and rinsed
½ cup broccoli, washed and cut into florets
½ cup red onion, chopped
½ cup yellow bell peppers, cubed
¼ cup walnuts, chopped

To serve:

1 tablespoon nutritional yeast

Preparation:

Place the dressing ingredients into a large mixing bowl and whisk together until thoroughly combined.

Add in the kale and use your hands to massage in the dressing for at least 1 minute; this step helps to soften the sometimes tough vegetable and infuse it with flavour.

Finally, add in the rest of the ingredients. Toss, then sprinkle with nutritional yeast and serve.

Autumn

Salads and Soups

WARM BROCCOLI NOODLE SALAD

For some reason, I keep buying these soy-marinated tempeh pieces, even though I don't like them very much! Thankfully I do love to challenge myself to create something delicious (or at least edible) from whatever I have in the fridge, and this recipe, another one of my strange concoctions, turned out to be a success.

Ingredients:

1 tablespoon olive oil
150 grams broccoli, chopped into smallish florets
150 grams Brussels sprouts, washed and halved
150 grams kale, washed and chopped
1 red chilli, deseeded and finely chopped
100 grams soy-marinated tempeh pieces
50 grams peanuts, roasted
4 wholemeal noodle nests (approx. 200 grams)
1 lime, squeezed
2 teaspoons vegan fish sauce
2 teaspoons soy sauce
1 large handful coriander, chopped

Preparation:

Over medium heat, sauté the vegetables, the chilli and the tempeh in the olive oil until vegetables start to soften.

Cook the noodles in boiling water for 5 minutes. Drain and add to the vegetables.

Add in sauces, lime juice and peanuts. Stir and serve warm.

FREEKEH SOUP

Freekeh, or roasted green wheat, may lend this soup its unphotogenic greenish-grey hue, but it's also what makes it so deliciously smoky and fragrant. Nutritious and filling to boot, it's the perfect dish for cool autumn nights.

For the Freekeh Soup:

1 tablespoon olive oil
2 onions, diced
2 cloves garlic, crushed
1 teaspoon Seven Spices (see note)
¼ teaspoon cumin
1 cup freekeh, washed and drained
4 cups vegetable stock
salt and pepper, to taste

To Serve:

1 lemon, chopped into wedges

Preparation:

In a saucepan set over medium heat, sauté the onion in the olive oil for 1 minute. Add in the garlic and spices and fry for another 30 seconds or so, until fragrant.

Add in the freekeh and vegetable stock, then stir and bring to a simmer. Cover and set heat to low.

Leave to cook for 20 minutes, then try the freekeh; if it's still a little chewy, return to heat and cook for another 10 minutes.

Taste and adjust seasoning, then serve alongside lemon wedges to squeeze into each bowl.

Note:

Seven Spices can be purchased pre-mixed or made at home by combining the following:

1 tablespoon ground allspice
2 tablespoons ground black pepper
½ tablespoon ground cinnamon
1 teaspoon ground cloves
1 ½ teaspoons ground cumin
1 tablespoon ground nutmeg
1 ½ teaspoons roasted ground cardamom

Mix well then store in an airtight container or spice jar, and use to make more recipes from this book!

Dips and Sides

PEČENE PAPRIKE (ROASTED PEPPERS)

This dish always transports me back to early autumn visits to my grandmother's country. People would gather their harvest of peppers and roast them over hot coal fires at twilight, scenting the air with a mouthwatering sweet smokiness as we rushed to our warm homes of an evening.

Ingredients:

1 kg long pointed red peppers, washed and dried
4 - 6 cloves garlic, peeled and chopped
3 tablespoons olive oil
3 tablespoons vinegar

Preparation:

Preheat the oven at 250°C.

Roast the peppers for 20 - 30 minutes until they soften and their skin starts to char.

Remove your peppers from the oven. While still hot, pile them into a bowl and cover with kitchen towels to trap in steam; this will make peeling them a lot easier.

Let sit for about 10 minutes, then peel the skin off the peppers; it should now come off easily. Once peeled, transfer peppers to a serving dish along with any accumulated juices.

In a bowl, combine garlic, olive oil, vinegar, half a teaspoon of salt and a sprinkle of black pepper. Pour over your peeled peppers and serve immediately, or store in an airtight container in the fridge for up to a week.

Note:

You can also grill the peppers over a barbecue.

Peel them over a bowl to make sure you don't lose any juice; it's half of what makes this dish so delicious.

Like to live dangerously? Roast some chilies along with your peppers and serve them together.

Autumn

Mains

MUJADDARA (RICE WITH LENTILS)

Another of my mother's recipes, this dish, both delicate and hearty, exudes comfort. The combination of rice and lentils also makes it an excellent source of protein.

Ingredients:

1 cup brown lentils, washed
2 cups water
1 large onion, peeled and halved
1 carrot, peeled
3 cloves garlic
1 bay leaf
parsley bouquet garni
1 cup basmati rice
3 onions, sliced thinly
3 tablespoons olive oil
1 vegetable stock cube
1 teaspoon Seven Spices (see Freekeh Soup for recipe)
1 teaspoon cumin (optional)
salt and pepper to taste

Preparation:

Place the water, lentils, onion halves, carrot, herbs and garlic in a saucepan. Bring to a boil and simmer for 20 minutes.

Once the lentils are cooked, fish them out using a small sieve and set aside, leaving the liquid and aromatics to simmer gently in the pot.

Soak the rice in cold water for 20 minutes, then drain.

Meanwhile, fry the sliced onions in the olive oil in a large pot set over medium-low heat, until golden brown.

Once the onions are done, use a slotted spoon to set aside two thirds of them on a paper towel for garnish, leaving the remaining onions in the pot. Add in the spices and fry until fragrant, approximately 30 seconds. Finally, add in the drained rice and cooked lentils, and stir until combined.

Remove aromatics from the lentil water then add in your stock cube, stirring until dissolved. Bring to a boil.

Autumn

Mains

Pour the hot cooking liquid over the lentils and rice, then taste and adjust seasoning. Check liquid level; it should cover the rice by about one centimetre. Top up with a splash of hot water if necessary.

Bring back to a boil, cover and cook over low heat for 15 minutes or a little longer, until rice is tender.

Garnish with reserved fried onions and pine nuts, and serve alongside salads and dips.

CREAMY MUSHROOM PASTA BAKE

A most delicious and comforting dish. I started making it when I was a teenager as a pasta dish, which you can do of course. More recently I made the pasta dish then topped it with cheese and baked it till a golden crispy top formed. Heaven!

For the Creamy Mushroom Pasta Bake:

300 grams dry pasta (a short shape works best here)
1 pot single cream (approx. 150 ml), labelled suitable for cooking

1 tablespoon olive oil
1 onion, chopped finely
4 cloves garlic, minced
1 punnet mushrooms, sliced
salt and pepper, to taste
1 pinch of smoked paprika
1 handful pine nuts, fried till golden and crunchy
1 handful grated cheddar
1 cup grated parmesan, divided

To Serve:

1 teaspoon chopped parsley

Preparation:

Preheat your oven at 180°C and prepare the pasta al dente according to packet instructions.

While the pasta is cooking, heat the olive oil in a frying pan, then cook the onion on low heat for 1 minute. Add the minced garlic and sliced mushrooms. Season with smoked paprika, salt and pepper, then sauté for a further 2 minutes. Stir in the cream, the pine nuts and half the parmesan.

Add in the drained pasta and stir to coat, then pour into baking dish. Top with grated cheddar and the rest of the parmesan, finish with a pinch of smoked paprika and bake in preheated oven for 25 minutes. Serve topped with a sprinkle of parsley.

Autumn

Mains

SALONI'S SPINACH AND PANEER

Everyone needs a friend like Saloni; the kind of friend you can talk to for hours and tell everything. My dearest, bestest friend. She lives in Dubai and we don't get to see each other as often as we'd like, but she always makes sure my favourite dish is on the table waiting for me when I do visit.

Ingredients:

10 cups spinach, roughly chopped
2 tablespoons olive oil
¾ cup onions, minced
4 garlic cloves, grated
1 inch piece of ginger, grated
2 green chillies, minced
½ teaspoon turmeric powder
¾ cup fresh tomato pulp
1 teaspoon garam masala

Preparation:

Blanch the spinach in boiling water for 2-3 minutes. Drain and blend to a smooth purée.

In a large saucepan, heat olive oil and fry onions over medium heat until translucent. Then add in the garlic, ginger, chillies and turmeric, sautéing for one minute.

Add tomato pulp and stir for another minute before adding puréed spinach. Cook for 2 minutes, then add garam masala and salt to taste, mixing well.

Gently stir in the paneer and allow to simmer for 2 more minutes. Serve hot with plain basmati rice.

Autumn

Mains

SPINACH FATAYER

These spinach pastries are eaten all across the Middle East, where I grew up, but funnily enough, I didn't actually run into one until a family trip to Canada, of all places. A growing teenager deprived of her daily rations of tabbouleh, I quickly became obsessed with them – I think they were all I ate the whole time I was there!

Yields approximately 35 spinach pastries

For the pastry:

3 cups plain flour
½ teaspoon salt
1 teaspoon yeast
½ cup of lukewarm water
½ cup of milk
½ cup of olive oil
¼ cup water to keep your hands wet whilst kneading the dough

For the filling:

1 kg of fresh spinach, washed and finely chopped
5 onions, finely chopped
2 tablespoons sumac
2 tablespoons lemon juice
4 tablespoons olive oil
1 tablespoon salt

Preparation:

In a measuring jug, sprinkle the yeast over the warm water; it should start to bubble slightly.

Sieve the flour onto the worktop, then stir in the salt. Form a well in the middle.
Add the milk and olive oil to the yeast and water.

Once combined, pour the liquid into the well in the flour and mix it in little by little, until all of the flour is incorporated.

When no dry flour remains, knead the dough for 20 minutes until it becomes elastic and stops sticking to the countertop, using the extra water as needed.

Transfer the dough ball to a greased bowl, cover and allow to rest in a warm place until doubled in size, for about an hour.

Autumn

Meanwhile, prepare the filling. Salt the chopped onions and leave to wilt for 10 minutes, then squeeze out excess liquid.

Combine the spinach and onions, then add sumac, olive oil, lemon juice and mix well. Taste filling and adjust seasoning accordingly.

Preheat the oven to 180°C. Punch down the risen dough and knead for about 2 minutes before dividing into thirty-five balls around the size of an egg. Cover with a cloth until needed.

Roll out a pastry ball until it is roughly the diameter of a saucer. Place a tablespoon of the spinach mixture into the centre and then fold the excess pastry inwards to form a triangle, sealing the dough by pinching the edges together.

Bake for 20 minutes.

Dessert, Sweet Treats and Baking

BAJADERE

Visiting my grandmother as a child, I remember being very scared of her downstairs neighbour, Bojana. My sister and I would be playing, making a ruckus, and whenever she came to knock on the door to complain, we would turn deathly quiet with fright! But she must have been trying to make an effort, because she invited us over once, and she had made these gorgeous layered chocolate bites that I'd only ever seen in cafés before. What magic was this? So I gathered up all of my courage and asked for her recipe, one I still have to this day.

Ingredients:

100 ml water
200 grams chocolate
200 grams walnuts, finely ground
200 grams Petit Beurre biscuits, finely ground
250 grams sugar
250 grams butter

Preparation:

Line a square or rectangular pan with baking paper.

In a saucepan mix water and sugar, then bring to boil until well dissolved and starting to thicken.

Add butter, stirring until melted, then ground walnuts until combined. Finally, stir in the biscuits.

Divide biscuit mixture in two and reserve one half. Pour the other half into your lined pan and press it out to form one even layer. Chill to set.

Meanwhile, melt half of your chocolate (100 g), then add to remaining biscuit mixture, stirring well until thoroughly combined.

Pour the chocolate and biscuit mixture into the lined pan and press evenly over your first layer. Return to fridge until cool.

Melt the remaining chocolate and pour it over your first two layers, using a spatula to create a smooth surface. Chill for 1–2 hours, until completely set, then lift the baking paper out of the pan and slice into rectangles before serving.

Autumn

Dessert, Sweet Treats and Baking

GIANT CHUNKY CHOCOLATE CHIP COOKIES

It is a fact universally known that no cookbook is complete without chocolate chip cookies. These are delicious and you can use your choice of chocolate chips - white chocolate, milk chocolate or dark (or mix them up if you like, they're your cookies!).

Ingredients:

75 grams granulated sugar
100 grams light brown sugar
125 grams unsalted butter, room temperature
1 large egg
½ teaspoon vanilla extract
300 grams plain flour
½ teaspoon bicarbonate of soda
1 ½ teaspoons baking powder
1 pinch of sea salt
200 grams chocolate chips

Preparation:

Cream together the sugars and butter, until the mixture has lightened in colour and increased in volume.

Add in the egg and vanilla extract, stirring until homogenous.

In a separate bowl, combine all the dry ingredients, then stir into the butter, sugar and egg mixture a little at a time until incorporated.

Pour in chocolate chips and knead them into the dough.

Split the dough into six portions and roll into large balls. Refrigerate for at least 2 hours, or up to two days.

Whenever you want freshly-baked cookies, simply preheat your oven to 180°C, then place on a lined baking tray, making sure to space them at least two inches apart from each other. Bake for 12 minutes.

Autumn

AUTUMN SEASON FOOD PLANNING

September till December
Seasonal vegetables and fruits

Aubergine, Apples, Beetroot, Blackberries, Broccoli, Carrots, Cauliflower, Celery, Chillies, Zucchini, Cucumber, Kale, Leeks, Lettuce, Onions, Potatoes, Radishes, Rocket, Spinach, Sweetcorn, Tomatoes, Watercress, Mushrooms, White Cabbage, Walnuts.

Shopping List

Item	Qty

Autumn Weekly Planner

Week 1	Week 2	Week 3	Week 4

Social Activities and recipe info

Brunches, dinner parties, family get-together, friends staying over

Recipes to try, comments and aide memoire

Notes

Autumn Menu Planner

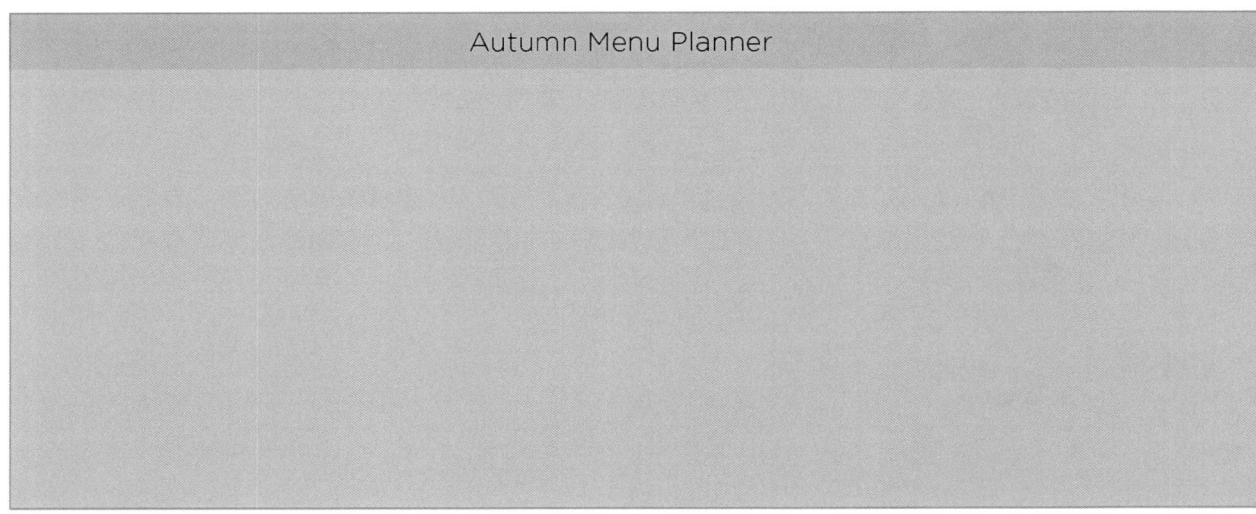

AUTUMN SEASON FOOD PLANNING

September till December
Seasonal vegetables and fruits

Aubergine, Apples, Beetroot, Blackberries, Broccoli, Carrots, Cauliflower, Celery, Chillies, Zucchini, Cucumber, Kale, Leeks, Lettuce, Onions, Potatoes, Radishes, Rocket, Spinach, Sweetcorn, Tomatoes, Watercress, Mushrooms, White Cabbage, Walnuts.

Autumn Weekly Planner

Week 1	Week 2	Week 3	Week 4

Social Activities and recipe info

Brunches, dinner parties, family get-together, friends staying over

Recipes to try, comments and aide memoire

Shopping List

Item	Qty

Notes

Autumn Menu Planner

Salads and Soups

CABBAGE SALAD

This was a staple on our dining table when I was growing up. Every time I make it for dinner parties my friends ask for the recipe. Crunchy and light, this moreish salad makes a fantastic alternative to coleslaw.

Ingredients:

1 head white cabbage, washed
1–3 cloves garlic, minced
2 lemons, squeezed
4 tablespoons olive oil
salt and pepper to taste
paprika (optional)

Preparation:

Finely slice the cabbage and place it in a bowl with the lemon juice, olive oil, salt and pepper; stir to combine. Leave to sit for at least 1 hour before serving. You may wish to top the dish with a sprinkle of paprika.

Salads and Soups

ADDAS (LENTIL SOUP)

When winter draws in, my mum would make this delicious soup regularly. It's earthy, scrumptious and fills the house with its delicious aroma. A classic winter treat.

Ingredients:

2 tablespoons olive oil
1 carrot, diced
1 onion, diced
1 potato, diced
250 grams split red lentils, washed
750 millilitres water, divided
1 vegetable stock cube
¼ teaspoon turmeric
½ teaspoon cumin
salt and pepper

Preparation:

In a large saucepan, heat the olive oil and gently sauté the vegetables over medium-low heat until soft. Add the washed lentils and 600 ml of water, bring to a simmer and cook over medium heat for 20 minutes, until lentils are soft.

Stir the stock cube into the remaining water (150 ml) until well dissolved. Add the stock to the soup, along with the turmeric, cumin and black pepper. Taste and adjust seasoning if necessary.

Enjoy as is or blend for a smoother texture.

Serve with fried pita bread or croutons and garnish with chopped parsley.

Salads and Soups

VEGETABLE SOUP

Ingredients:

1 tablespoon olive oil
1 large onion, peeled and chopped finely
2 cloves of garlic, peeled and chopped finely
2 medium potatoes, peeled and cut into cubes no larger than 1 cm
2 medium carrots, peeled and cut into cubes no larger than 1 cm
2 zucchini, washed and cut into cubes no larger than 1 cm
½ cup peas
2 cubes vegetable stock, dissolved in 1 ½ litres hot water
1 tablespoon chopped parsley, to serve

Preparation:

In a large saucepan, sauté the onions and garlic in the olive oil over a low heat for 1 minute, add the carrots and sauté for 1 more minute.

Add in the rest of the vegetables (save for the parsley), followed by the water and stock cubes. Bring to a boil and simmer for 10 minutes, until the vegetables are almost cooked.

Finally, drop in the fresh noodles or dumplings if using (see recipe below). Simmer for a few more minutes, till cooked through. Serve sprinkled with parsley.

Salads and Soups

SOUP NOODLES AND DUMPLINGS

My grandmother had a neighbour and dear friend, Moka. She and her husband George took me in as their honorary grandchild after my grandmother's passing, and this recipe, along with many others in this book, came from her kitchen. Should you make these noodles or dumplings, you can just drop them into your vegetable soup.

Ingredients:

1 ½ - 2 cups plain flour
2 egg yolks
a pinch of salt

Preparation:

Mix together the flour and salt, then make a well and place in your egg yolk. Combine with a fork until a dough is formed.

Flour your countertop then roll out your dough as thinly as possible using a rolling pin. Once thin enough, gently flour the surface of the dough before rolling it over itself like a cigar.

Slice into thin strips with a sharp knife. Leave to air dry for about 30 minutes, then drop into your pot of soup until cooked, approximately 3–5 minutes.

You can also use the same method (and a little less flour) to make dough for knedleh (dumplings).

Form the dough into small balls using a spoon and drop into boiling soup. Cook for around 1 minute, or until dumplings rise to the surface.

Mains

AUBERGINE FATTEH

There is something special about fatteh, some kind of delicious alchemy that occurs between its layers when they meet. Perhaps that's why it's a special occasion dish! Though it is traditionally eaten during Ramadan, I like to make it for Christmas.

Ingredients:

olive oil
3 medium aubergines, cubed
1 onion, diced
2 cloves garlic, crushed
1 cup vegetable stock
1 teaspoon pomegranate molasses
2 tablespoons tomato paste

For the sauce:

2 cups plain yogurt
½ lemon
3–4 cloves of garlic, crushed
salt to taste

To serve:

pita bread, cut into cubes and fried in olive oil till crisp and golden
1 handful pine nuts, toasted
chopped parsley for garnish (optional)

Preparation:

First, salt and fry aubergine cubes in olive oil until golden. Set aside.

In a saucepan, sauté the onion over medium heat in a little olive oil for 1 minute, then add in your garlic and stir.

Add the aubergine cubes, followed by the pomegranate molasses, tomato paste and stock. Stir, turn the heat down to low and cover, leaving to simmer for 5–10 minutes.

Meanwhile, in a bowl, combine the yogurt, lemon juice, garlic and salt. Set aside.

To serve, first scatter the fried pita over a serving platter, then spoon on the warm aubergine mixture, followed by the yogurt sauce.

Garnish with pine nuts and parsley and enjoy hot, warm or cold.

Mains

MAALOUBEH

The name of this dish translates to 'upside-down', because once cooked it is turned out onto a platter like a cake. This rather risky step somehow makes it all taste so much better, perhaps thanks to the relief one feels when the whole thing doesn't end up on the floor! Refined yet theatrical, it's the perfect centrepiece in a Christmas meal.

Ingredients:

2 beef tomatoes, sliced (see note)
1 aubergine, cut into thick slices and fried till golden
1 cauliflower, cut into largish florets and fried till golden
2 potatoes, sliced into thick slices and fried till golden
1 whole head garlic, peeled
2 teaspoons Seven Spices (see Freekeh Soup for recipe)
½ teaspoon cinnamon
2 cups rice, washed and soaked in cold water for at least an hour
4 cups vegetable stock, hot
pine nuts, roasted till golden and crunchy

Preparation:

Layer all the vegetables at the bottom of a large pot, starting with the tomatoes, making sure to season each layer liberally with spices, salt and interspersed garlic cloves.

Place the pot over medium-low heat, pour in half of the hot vegetable stock and bring to a simmer. Cook for 3 minutes.

Add in the washed rice, remaining stock, spices and one more sprinkle of salt. Cover the pot with a tight lid and leave to simmer over low heat for 30 minutes, until all the stock has been absorbed and the rice is fluffy and well-cooked.

Carefully turn the dish out onto a platter, scatter with pine nuts and serve alongside yoghurt cucumber salad.

Note:

The tomatoes in maaloubeh quite literally take the heat for the other vegetables: they will burn and stick to the bottom of the pot, but everything else should remain unscathed thanks to their sacrifice.

Winter

Mains

VOJNIČKI PASULJ (ARMY BEANS)

A member of my family served as a nurse in World War II, and was awarded a medal for Services to the Nation for her life-saving work. This is a recipe from those days, a hearty, comforting meal that's also cheap to make and easy to scale should you need to feed an army.

Ingredients:

500 grams dry white beans
1 onion, finely chopped
4 cloves garlic, crushed
1 carrot, grated
100 grams olive oil
2 tablespoons plain flour
1 tablespoon paprika or smoked paprika
1 bay leaf
1 dried chilli, soaked in cold water for a couple of hours
1 vegetable stock cube
salt and pepper to taste
1 tablespoon chopped parsley

Preparation:

Leave the beans to soak overnight in a large volume of cold water, making sure they are covered by at least two inches; the beans will swell as they absorb the water.

The next day, discard the soaking liquid and place the beans in a large pot. Cover with cold water, bring to a boil and let cook for 15 minutes, then discard the cooking liquid again. Cover the beans with boiling water and add in half the garlic and onion. Allow to cook over medium heat, topping up with hot water as needed.

In a separate saucepan, over low heat, sauté together the remainder of the onion as well as the carrot in half of your olive oil. Fry until soft and light golden in colour.

Once the beans are halfway cooked, add in the fried vegetables, dried chilli and bay leaf, keeping your stirring to a minimum to avoid mashing the beans.

Warm up the rest of the olive oil in your now empty saucepan, then add in the flour and fry until it takes on a light golden colour. Remove from the heat then add in the other half of the

Mains

crushed garlic and the paprika, stirring until very well combined.

Once the beans are cooked and soft, stir in the vegetable stock cube until dissolved, then add salt to taste. Finally, add in the flour mixture over very low heat, stirring gently to ensure that it thickens nicely without curdling or separating.

Cook for a further 20 - 30 minutes, then remove from heat, taste for salt and finish with a sprinkle of black pepper. Top with chopped parsley and serve over white rice.

MACEDONIAN PIE

I learned this recipe by making it with Moka, my grandmother's neighbour. She and her husband George had an allotment, which he would go to visit every day, coming home with a basketful of vegetables he'd traded for or grown himself. Of course there were no mobile phones in those days, so he couldn't call ahead to tell her what he got; she simply had to wait to be presented with the day's harvest then come up with dinner on the spot. This pie can be prepared with a variety of fillings, which makes it perfectly suited to this kind of situation!

For the dough:

1 cake fresh yeast or 1 sachet dried yeast
2 cups lukewarm water
½ teaspoon sugar
750 grams plain flour, sieved
1 teaspoon salt
250 grams butter, softened (add more if needed)

For the filling:
2 cups vegetables of your choice (see note)
1 tablespoon butter
salt and pepper to taste

Preparation:

Stir the sugar into the lukewarm water then crumble or sprinkle in your yeast and set aside. In a large bowl, add the salt to half the flour (325 g) and combine.

Pour the yeast and water mixture into the other half of the flour, stirring with a wooden spoon until well combined. Add in the flour and salt mix, stirring until a dough is formed, then cover and leave to rest in a warm place for one hour.

Meanwhile, prepare the filling: sauté your vegetables in the butter over medium heat until soft. Season to taste and set aside.

Once rested, knead the dough until elastic and less sticky. Roll out over a floured counter, generously spread with butter then fold over. Repeat this step three to four times.

Preheat the oven at 200°C. Butter a baking dish and lay in the dough, stretching it to size, then leave to rise for another 30 minutes.

Top with filling then fold over the edges. Place in the oven and bake until golden brown, checking often and lowering the temperature if necessary to make sure it doesn't start to burn.

> **Note:**
>
> Moka made this with sautéed leeks, but it would also be delicious with other fillings, like mushroom and onion or diced carrots, potatoes and peas.
>
> If you would prefer for your pie to have a lid, set aside half the buttered dough. Proceed with the recipe as written, then roll out the second half of the dough and place on top of the filling, seal at the edges and bake.

Dessert, Sweet Treats and Baking

STRAWBERRY AND CHOCOLATE CAKE

For the cake layers:

2 ¼ cups plain flour
¾ cup cocoa
1 teaspoon salt
1 ¼ teaspoons baking soda
¼ teaspoon baking powder
1 ⅔ cups sugar
¾ cup melted butter, cooled
2 eggs
1 ¼ cups water
1 teaspoon vanilla extract
3 tablespoons grated chocolate

To assemble:

1 bowl prepared Chantilly cream (see Raspberry Sherry Trifle for recipe)
1 punnet strawberries, washed and sliced
6 chocolate-dipped strawberries
1 tablespoon grated chocolate

Preparation:

Preheat the oven to 180°C and generously grease and flour two eight-inch round layer cake tins.

Place all of the cake ingredients save for the grated chocolate in the bowl of a stand mixer set to a low speed for 30 seconds. Scrape down the sides of the bowl to ensure no dry ingredients remain.

Set your mixer to high for 2 minutes, then sprinkle in the grated chocolate and mix for another 30 seconds, until incorporated.

Divide the batter between your two cake tins and bake for 30 - 35 minutes, until a wooden toothpick inserted in the centre comes out clean. Allow the cakes to cool in their tins for a few minutes before removing them, then turn them out and leave to cool on wire racks.

To assemble, set the first cake on your serving platter, spread with a generous layer of Chantilly cream, and arrange the sliced strawberries on top. Stack on the second cake layer then cover the top and sides of the cake with the remaining Chantilly. Decorate with chocolate shavings and chocolate-dipped strawberries and chill until ready to serve.

Winter

Dessert, Sweet Treats and Baking

BROWN SODA BREAD

This recipe came to me from the brilliant Mary Kerins, who I met back when I was working for the British Airport Authority and she the Dublin Airport Authority. We got to know each other over the course of several policy meetings across Europe, quite a long time ago now, and became good friends. We haven't seen each other in person for years, but we've stayed in touch and call each other once a month for coffee and a chat. I love soda bread, and her version is no exception!

Ingredients:

8 ounces (½ pound) plain flour
1 pound wholemeal flour (I use extra-coarse)
2 teaspoons bicarbonate of soda
1 teaspoon baking powder
a pinch of salt
3 tablespoons vegetable oil
1 egg
1.5–2 pints buttermilk or plain yoghurt

Preparation:

Preheat oven to 170°C.

Place all dry ingredients in a large bowl and combine well.

Add in oil, buttermilk or yoghurt and beaten egg, mixing with a wooden spoon until it forms a sloppy dough. It will look wrong but is right!

Transfer to an eight-inch loaf tin lined with baking paper and bake for 45 minutes.

Drink

HEALTHY METABOLISM ACTIVATING LEMON GINGER TONIC TEA

Over the past few years, I've become more interested in ginger and turmeric's immune-boosting properties and tried to add more of both to my diet. This is a wonderfully warming way to do so.

Ingredients:

1 peppermint tea bag
¼ cup fresh mint leaves
juice of one lemon
1 teaspoon minced ginger
1 teaspoon minced turmeric root
1 teaspoon apple cider vinegar
1 litre water
honey (optional)

Preparation:

Place all the ingredients into a saucepan and bring to a low simmer for five or so minutes.

Leave to cool a little and serve in a mug. For a little sweetness, try it with a splash of honey.

WINTER SEASON FOOD PLANNING

December till March
Seasonal vegetables and fruits

Beetroot, Carrots, Celery, Kale, Leeks, Mushrooms, Onions, White Cabbage. Potatoes

Shopping List

Item	Qty

Winter Weekly Planner

Week 1	Week 2	Week 3	Week 4

Social Activities and recipe info

Brunches, dinner parties, family get-together, friends staying over

Recipes to try, comments and aide memoire

Notes

Winter Menu Planner

WINTER SEASON FOOD PLANNING

December till March
Seasonal vegetables and fruits

Beetroot, Carrots, Celery, Kale, Leeks, Mushrooms, Onions, White Cabbage. Potatoes

Winter Weekly Planner

Week 1	Week 2	Week 3	Week 4

Social Activities and recipe info

Brunches, dinner parties, family get-together, friends staying over

Recipes to try, comments and aide memoire

Shopping List

Item	Qty

Notes

Winter Menu Planner

SPRING

Salads and Soups

FATTOUSH

Fattoush is a delicious, zingy salad that's also the perfect way to use up whatever is in your vegetable drawer. Its tart dressing and crispy pita croutons make it absolutely irresistible.

For the salad:

1 cucumber, peeled and cubed
2 large ripe tomatoes, diced
1 head gem lettuce, cut into wide strips
1 green or red pepper, cubed
2 cooked beetroots, cubed
1 handful radishes, quartered
1 handful whole mint leaves

For the dressing:

2 tablespoons pomegranate molasses
4 tablespoons extra-virgin olive oil
½ lemon, squeezed
1 tablespoon sumac (optional)
salt to taste

To serve:

3 pita breads, cut into squares and fried in olive oil till golden

Preparation:

Whisk the dressing ingredients together in a small bowl until combined.

Place the vegetables in a salad bowl, then pour over the dressing. Toss to coat and add fried pita. Serve immediately.

Note:

This recipe is merely a starting point; feel free to adjust the vegetables to your preference.

Spring

Dips and Sides

TAHINI DIP

Easy, quick and requiring very few ingredients, this versatile recipe is well worth making. It's bright and nutritious yet still decadently creamy, and works equally well as a dipping sauce or salad dressing.

Ingredients:

½ cup tahini
½ lemon, squeezed
1 tablespoon olive oil
salt and pepper to taste

Preparation:

In a bowl, combine the ingredients, stirring continuously. The tahini will thicken before it relaxes, and the mixture will seem like it's seizing up; this is normal. Carry on stirring until the sauce homogenises, then taste and adjust seasoning.

Note:

This is also delicious when made with crushed garlic or finely chopped parsley.

Mains

ITALIAN AUBERGINE BAKE (PARMIGIANA)

My mother has always loved Italy, and she instilled that love in me through yearly trips we took there as a family. I don't get to go nearly as often now, but I remain a fan of the culture, people, language and cuisine. They just do it better over there, and this dish is no exception!

For the dressing:

3 large aubergines, sliced
2 tablespoons olive oil
1 large onion, diced
2 cloves of garlic, minced
1 mild red chilli, minced
1 bottle passata
10 basil leaves
Parmesan, grated
1 ball mozzarella, torn

Preparation:

Preheat the oven at 200°C.

Generously salt and pepper your aubergine slices and roast for 25 minutes.

In a large pan, sauté the onion and garlic over medium heat until translucent and slightly golden. Season with salt and pepper and add in minced chilli. Fry for 1 more minute, stirring continuously, before pouring in the passata. Stir in the basil.

Spread a layer of sauce in a large baking dish. Follow with Parmesan and a layer of aubergine slices.

Repeat until you have three layers. Finally, top the dish with mozzarella and Parmesan.

Bake in your preheated oven for 30 minutes until golden and bubbling hot.

Mains

BROADBEAN MAALOUBEH

A green twist on maaloubeh, this dish is a wonderful way to ring in spring.

Ingredients:

olive oil
10 cloves garlic, peeled and left whole
3 tablespoons chopped coriander
1 packet frozen broad beans (approx. 2 ½ cups or 500 grams)
4 cups vegetable stock, very hot
2 cups rice, washed and soaked in cold water for at least an hour
2 teaspoons Seven Spices (see *Freekeh Soup* for recipe)
pine nuts, roasted till golden and crunchy

Preparation:

Warm the olive oil in a large pot and fry the garlic and coriander for 30 seconds over medium heat. Add in the broad beans and sauté for a further 5 minutes.

Pour in one and a half cups of the vegetable stock and leave to simmer for 3 minutes, then add the washed rice, remaining stock and spices.

Cover the pot with a tight lid and leave to simmer for 30 minutes, until all the stock has been absorbed and the rice is cooked and fluffy.

Carefully turn the dish out onto a platter, scatter with the pine nuts and serve with yoghurt.

Mains

YOGHURT PASTA

My version of this classic Middle-Eastern pasta dish replaces the meat with mushrooms for a tangy, tasty meal that comes together in minutes.

For the dressing:

300 grams dry pasta, any shape you like
1 pot full-fat greek yoghurt (approx. 500 grams)
10 cloves of garlic, minced
1 onion, finely chopped
1 punnet mushrooms, minced
1 heaped teaspoon Seven Spices (see Freekeh Soup for recipe)
½ teaspoon cumin
1 tablespoon chopped parsley or basil
1 handful pine nuts, fried till golden
salt and pepper, to taste

Preparation:

Cook pasta as per packet instructions. Meanwhile, fry the onion over low heat for 1 minute in a little olive oil. Add in the minced mushrooms, season with salt and pepper and sauté for a further 5 minutes, until all liquid has evaporated.

In a separate pan, sauté the garlic for a minute over low heat, stirring constantly, then add in the spices and fry until fragrant.

Season with salt then pour in the yoghurt, stirring constantly. Keep stirring as you wait for the sauce to come to a gentle simmer for 1 minute.

Stir in your herb of choice, followed by the pasta. Serve topped with the mushrooms, pine nuts and a sprinkle of chopped herbs.

Spring

Mains

FUL MUDAMMAS

Another of my mother's recipes, this dish was a firm favourite in our household growing up. I remember its comforting aroma wafting through the house when she would whip up a batch for breakfast on Friday mornings, or for a quick and easy dinner. It's perfect eaten with pita and a hot cup of sweet tea.

Ingredients:

3 tablespoons olive oil
3 cloves garlic
2 tablespoons tomato paste mixed into ½ cup of hot water
1 tablespoon chopped parsley
2 cans fava beans, drained and rinsed
1 pinch salt and pepper
1 tomato, chopped
1 onion, finely chopped
1 tablespoon chopped parsley
1 red chilli chopped finely (optional garnish if you like heat)

Preparation:

Fry the garlic in the olive oil over medium heat then add in the fava beans and the diluted tomato paste. Season to taste with salt and pepper, then bring to a boil and simmer for 2–3 minutes.

Pour into a serving bowl and garnish with chopped onion, tomato and parsley.

Spring

Dessert, Sweet Treats and Baking

CHEESE BOARD

In the opening scene to the Mission Impossible franchise, Tom Cruise's character is relaxing in first class on a British Airways flight when he is handed his titular mission, should he choose to accept it. The specifics of which airline he was flying with may seem insignificant to most, but as a BA employee when the film first came out, I was thrilled to recognise it! I too was on a British Airways flight when I was confronted with a life-changing moment: my first cheese board. I did choose to accept that mission, and have loved cheese boards ever since!

For the dressing:

stinking bishop cheese
mature cheddar
stilton
brie
grapes
celery sticks
carrot sticks
a selection of your favourite crackers

Preparation:

Arrange the cheeses, the crackers and the crudités on a wooden board. Serve alongside a bottle of fine port.

Dessert, Sweet Treats and Baking

KOCH
(SEMOLINA SPONGE CAKE)

The first time I saw Koch being prepared, I couldn't believe my eyes. How could such a marvellous dessert be so simple to make? Wholesome and not too sweet, this cake is like a little miracle.

Ingredients:

5 eggs
5 tablespoons sugar
5 tablespoons semolina
1 litre oat milk
1 teaspoon vanilla extract
Preheat oven at 200°C.

Preparation:

In a bowl, combine the eggs, sugar and semolina. Transfer to a greased cake tin.

Place in the preheated oven, lowering the temperature to 180°C once the cake starts to rise. Bake for approximately 25 minutes.

While the cake is baking, combine milk and vanilla extract into a saucepan and bring to a boil.

Take the cake out of the oven and immediately pour on the hot vanilla milk.

Leave to cool, then refrigerate. Enjoy once chilled.

Spring

Dessert, Sweet Treats and Baking

RASPBERRY SHERRY TRIFLE

I take great pride in my trifle, and with good reason: it's fantastic!

For the vanilla custard:

⅔ cup sugar
¼ cup cornstarch
½ teaspoon salt
3 cups milk
4 egg yolks
2 tablespoons butter
1 ½ tablespoon plus 1 teaspoon vanilla extract

For the Chantilly cream:

½ vanilla bean, split and scraped
1 cup whipping cream, very cold
2 tablespoons icing sugar
½ teaspoon vanilla extract

To assemble:

1 packet vegan raspberry jelly
1 packet sponge fingers
½ cup dry sherry
1 punnet raspberries, some set aside for garnish
chocolate shavings

Preparation:

First, prepare the vegan raspberry jelly according to packet instructions and place in the fridge to set.

To make the vanilla custard, lightly beat your egg yolks in a measuring jug. Combine the sugar, cornstarch and salt in a cold saucepan, then gradually add in the milk. Warm over low heat, stirring constantly, until the mixture starts to simmer and thicken, then let cook for 1 minute, still stirring.

Slowly pour half of the hot milk mixture into the beaten egg yolks, whisking vigorously, then pour back into the saucepan, still whisking. Bring back to a low simmer and let cook for 1 more minute, stirring continuously with a wooden spoon.

Remove from the heat and add in butter and vanilla. Cover and let cool, then refrigerate until chilled.

Dessert, Sweet Treats and Baking

Meanwhile, prepare the Chantilly cream. Scrape the vanilla seeds into a bowl with the cream and sugar and whip with an electric mixer until soft peaks form, approximately 3 minutes. Cover and refrigerate until needed.

To assemble the trifle, place the sponge fingers in a single layer at the bottom of your trifle dish. Drizzle the sponge fingers with half of the sherry, then repeat for another layer.

Scatter with most of the raspberries, then spoonfuls of the prepared jelly. Pour on the custard, then top with the Chantilly cream. Finally, decorate the top with chocolate shavings and the last of the raspberries.

Refrigerate until ready to serve.

Drink

TURKISH COFFEE

'A single cup of coffee is remembered for forty years,' or so goes the Turkish proverb. It must be true, because whenever I smell the fragrant aroma of the coffee brewing and hear the dainty cups clink against each other, I am reminded of my childhood, and taken right back to cozy mornings in bed, listening to my parents chat as they prepare for the day and drink their coffee together. I still get that lovely safe feeling every morning as I start the day with two cups of this coffee, basking in the ritual of its preparation.

Serves two:

3 heaped teaspoons Turkish coffee (see note)
sugar to taste
water

Preparation:

Measure out three small cups (see note) of water and pour into your pot. Let the water come to a simmer, then fill a coffee cup with the hot water. Set aside.

Add the ground Turkish coffee and sugar (to taste) to the pot. Stir and return to heat, until gently bubbling again. Watch it carefully at this stage, or it will try to boil out of the pot.

Once it starts to simmer and rise in the pot, remove from heat and pour in the water you set aside in the coffee cup.

Return the pot to the fire; allow the coffee to warm up and start to rise again, at which point it is ready. Divide between two cups and serve the traditional way, alongside tall glasses of ice cold water.

Note:

Turkish coffee can now easily be found online. I recommend Al Ameed; theirs comes in light, medium or dark roast, with or without cardamom. My personal favourite, medium roast with cardamom, makes a fantastically fragrant cup of coffee.

While this is traditionally made in a cezve, the long-handled copper pot specifically designed for this purpose, you could also make this in a small saucepan. It is usually drunk out of Arabian coffee cups, which are roughly the size of an espresso cup.

SPRING SEASON FOOD PLANNING

March till June
Seasonal vegetables and fruits

Beetroot, Carrots, Kale, Radishes, Rocket, Spinach, Aubergine, Chillies, Lettuce, Peppers, Rocket, Spinach, Spring Onions, Strawberries, Watercress. Mushrooms, Broad Beans, Broccoli, Cauliflower, Zucchini, Cucumber, Lettuce, Peppers, Radishes, Raspberries.

Spring Weekly Planner

Week 1	Week 2	Week 3	Week 4

Social Activities and recipe info

Brunches, dinner parties, family get-together, friends staying over

Recipes to try, comments and aide memoire

Shopping List

Item	Qty

Notes

Spring Menu Planner

SPRING SEASON FOOD PLANNING

March till June
Seasonal vegetables and fruits

Beetroot, Carrots, Kale, Radishes, Rocket, Spinach, Aubergine, Chillies, Lettuce, Peppers, Rocket, Spinach, Spring Onions, Strawberries, Watercress. Mushrooms, Broad Beans, Broccoli, Cauliflower, Zucchini, Cucumber, Lettuce, Peppers, Radishes, Raspberries.

Spring Weekly Planner

Week 1	Week 2	Week 3	Week 4

Social Activities and recipe info

Brunches, dinner parties, family get-together, friends staying over

Recipes to try, comments and aide memoire

Shopping List

	Item	Qty

Notes

Spring Menu Planner

SUMMER

Salads and Soups

TABBOULEH

During my teenage years, I went through a phase of being completely obsessed with tabbouleh. It was almost all I ate, and I would enjoy platefuls every day when I got home from school. Looking back, I wonder if this craving might have been my body's way of making sure I was getting enough iron after converting to vegetarianism! I'm still a fan of tabbouleh today, and I like it made just this way, with nutty, chewy bulgur and lots and lots of parsley.

For the Tabbouleh:

¾ cup bulgur (cracked wheat)
2 large bunches of parsley (approx. 200g), washed
1 small bunch mint, washed
2 large tomatoes
3 lemons, juiced
olive oil
salt and pepper to taste

To Serve:

1 lemon, chopped into wedges
gem lettuce leaves

Preparation:

Soak the bulgur in cold water for at least 30 minutes. Meanwhile, dice the tomatoes into small cubes, then chop the herbs very finely. Place in a large bowl.

Drain the bulgur, using your hands to squeeze out as much water as possible, then scatter into the bowl with the herbs and tomatoes.

Dress with lemon juice, olive oil and salt and pepper to taste.

Toss well to combine, and serve garnished with lemon wedges or spooned into gem lettuce leaves.

Summer

Salads and Soups

YOGURT CUCUMBER SALAD

A cousin to Greek tzatziki, this refreshing salad is a perfect complement to richly spiced rice dishes like makloubeh and mujaddara.

Ingredients:

2 cups plain yogurt
1 cucumber, halved lengthwise then finely sliced
2 cloves garlic, crushed
1 handful of mint leaves, finely chopped, some set aside for garnish
salt to taste

Preparation:

In a bowl, combine all of the ingredients. Taste and adjust seasoning as needed.

Decorate with the last of the mint and serve cold.

Summer

Dips and Sides

MOUTABAL (SMOKY AUBERGINE DIP)

This dish became a staple in my parents' house after my father was diagnosed with diabetes; someone must have recommended moutabbal to them as a low-carb option, because my mother learned how to make it for him. From then on, there was always some ready in the fridge, while more aubergines were already being roasted for the next batch.

Ingredients:

3 medium aubergines, washed
2 cloves garlic, crushed
3 tablespoons tahini
1 tablespoon pomegranate molasses
2 tablespoons lemon juice
olive oil
salt

Preparation:

Preheat oven to 200°C.

Bake whole aubergines for 30 - 40 minutes, until soft enough to yield when tested with a wooden spoon.

Turn off the oven and leave to cool with the door closed for 1 hour.

Carefully peel the aubergines by hand, trying to save as much of the flesh as possible; the closer it is to the burnt skin, the more smoky flavour it will impart to the final dish.

Roughly chop into large chunks, then knead by hand until the mixture takes on a creamy consistency.

Add garlic, tahini, pomegranate molasses and lemon juice, and combine. Finish with a drizzle of olive oil and salt to taste.

Garnish with a sprinkle of sumac and pomegranate seeds, and serve in dip bowls alongside crudités, crusty bread, pita or breadsticks.

Mains

VEGGIE DREAM STUFFED AUBERGINES

Middle Eastern cuisine has many elaborate stuffed vegetable dishes, but they can sometimes seem a bit daunting to make. So I came up with this much more beginner-friendly version, which does away with all the usual complexities of the stuffing while still producing delicious results.

Ingredients:

2 large aubergines
½ onion, diced
1 cup quinoa
4 tomatoes, chopped
2 tablespoons olive oil
½ teaspoon black pepper
1 handful of parsley, chopped
1 handful of mint leaves, chopped
salt to taste

For the tomato sauce:

1 tablespoon olive oil
1 medium onion, very finely sliced
1 garlic clove, coarsely chopped
400 grams (1 tin) good quality tinned tomatoes
2 vegetable stock cubes, dissolved in two cups of boiling water
1 handful parsley, chopped
a few mint leaves, chopped

Preparation:

Preheat oven to 200°C.

Cut the aubergines in half lengthwise, leaving the tops on. Scoop out the flesh with a spoon, then dice finely and set aside for the sauce.

Combine all filling ingredients and mix well.

Place aubergines cut side up on a baking dish and spoon in the filling.

In a bowl, combine all the ingredients for the tomato sauce.

To assemble, top each stuffed aubergine with two tablespoons of the sauce, then pour the remainder into the baking dish, making sure it reaches to the tops of the aubergines (top up with a splash of boiling water as needed).

Summer

Cover with foil and bake for about 30 minutes, until the aubergines are soft, then remove foil and bake for a further 10 minutes.

> **Notes:**
>
> The quinoa in this recipe can be replaced with an equal volume of rice if you prefer.
>
> This dish can also be made using zucchini or peppers instead of aubergines, or all three at once for variety!

Mains

GREEK ZUCCHINI SPAGHETTI

It never occurred to me Greek cuisine might feature pasta until a working lunch at a fabulous Greek restaurant in London. I ordered this dish because it was the only vegetarian main on the menu, but it blew me away! The lemon zest and feta make it quite a departure from the tomato and parmesan we're so used to seeing paired with spaghetti.

Ingredients:

1 tablespoon olive oil
2 small onions, sliced
6 cloves garlic, sliced
4 medium zucchini, cut into long strips
1 carrot cut into thin sticks, similar in size to the zucchini
1 tablespoon butter
300 grams spaghetti
salt and pepper to taste
1 lemon, zested and squeezed
50 grams pine nuts
100 grams feta cheese, crumbled
1 teaspoon chopped parsley

Preparation:

In a saucepan, sauté the onions in olive oil over low heat until translucent, about 5 minutes. Add the garlic and fry for 1 more minute.

Turn up the heat and add the courgette and carrot. Fry for 5–10 minutes, stirring frequently, until most of the moisture has evaporated.

Meanwhile, cook the spaghetti according to your own preferences and drain, reserving a small amount of the pasta water.

Turn the heat all the way down, add in the butter and put the lid on. Cook for 10 minutes, stirring occasionally, until the mixture is almost cooked (a little al dente crunch can be nice, but if that's not your thing, add another 5 minutes to the cooking time).

Place the pine nuts in a small frying pan over low heat and lightly toast them. Stir frequently and watch carefully to make sure they don't burn.

When the vegetables are done, add the salt, pepper, lemon zest and juice, pine nuts and a drizzle of pasta water to loosen.

Spoon on top of the spaghetti and scatter with crumbled feta and chopped parsley.

Summer

Mains

MINI PIZZAS

I used to sell homemade baked goods for a bit of spending money while I was in university, and I suppose if things had gone a little differently I could be running a café now. That isn't what happened, but I still have the recipes from those days. These mini pizzas were always a hit; deceptively easy and very delicious, they are the first thing to vanish from serving platters.

For the dough:

1 ½ cups warm water
1 tablespoon active dry yeast
2 tablespoons sugar
¼ cup olive oil
4 ½ cups strong bread flour
1 tablespoon salt

Your choice of toppings:

1 cup tomato sauce
4 cups mozzarella cheese, shredded
green pepper, diced
onion, diced
sweetcorn
mushrooms, thinly sliced
black olives, pitted
roasted artichokes, thinly sliced
zucchini, thinly sliced
Roquefort cheese, crumbled
figs, thinly sliced
caramelised onions
chilli flakes

Preparation:

Pour the warm water into a large mixing bowl, stir in the sugar and sprinkle the yeast on top. Allow to sit for 5 minutes; the yeast will start to foam and bubble.

Add the oil, flour and salt. Stir with a wooden spoon until a dough takes shape, then transfer to a lightly floured surface and knead for about 5 minutes. You should obtain a smooth dough. Transfer the dough ball to a greased bowl, cover, and allow to rest until doubled in size, for about an hour.

Set the oven to 250°C. While it preheats, line a baking sheet with parchment paper and brush with olive oil. Divide the dough into sixteen equal balls.

Flatten each ball into a thin circle roughly the size of a saucer and place on the parchment-covered baking sheet.

Spread sauce and sprinkle on toppings as desired.

Bake for 8 - 10 minutes, until the crust is crisp and the cheese is melted and lightly browned.

Note:

You can use whatever toppings you like, but I personally recommend the combination of crumbled Roquefort with sliced fig and caramelised onion.

Dessert, Sweet Treats and Baking

ALYZA'S WAFFLES

Another one of my dear friends, Alyza, had to be included in the book … but since she doesn't cook, and her husband does, this recipe is actually his!

Ingredients:

(Makes six waffles)

2 cups plain flour
1 tablespoon sugar
4 teaspoons baking powder
1 pinch of salt
2 eggs, whisked till light and fluffy
1 3/4 cups oat milk
1/2 cup olive oil
1 teaspoon vanilla extract

Preparation:

Place the dry ingredients into a large mixing bowl, then pour in the oat milk, olive oil and vanilla extract, mixing continuously. Once well incorporated, gently fold in the whisked eggs.

Pour batter onto the hot iron, cook until golden brown and the iron stops steaming (3–5 minutes). Repeat until all the batter is gone.

Serve hot with butter and maple syrup, strawberries and blueberries, Nutella and sliced bananas or even a scoop of ice cream.

Summer

Dessert, Sweet Treats and Baking

LAZY NO-BAKE CHOCOLATE CAKE

My brother was enrolled at the New English School while we were living in Jordan, and one day came home with the school cookbook, a compendium of some of the students' families best recipes. This was one of them, and I've never forgotten it! It's ideal for those summer days when turning on the oven feels unmanageable.

Ingredients:

150 grams Petit Beurre or Digestive biscuits
200 millilitres cream
100 grams butter, melted
100 grams sugar, or more to taste
100 grams cocoa powder
1 handful of fruit jelly candies, chopped (optional)

Preparation:

Crush biscuits and add in all remaining ingredients. Mix well, making sure everything is thoroughly combined.

Pour mixture onto a sheet of aluminium foil and roll it up into a log shape.

Refrigerate for 4 hours. To serve, remove foil and cut into slices.

Dessert, Sweet Treats and Baking

LUQAIMAT

I first fell in love with this Emirati delicacy after trying it at Emirates Palace. One is never enough, so I asked my dear friend Huda Al Houqani for her treasured family recipe for these golden nuggets. Dripping with date syrup and speckled with toasted sesame seeds, they gleam like jewels in Aladdin's cave of wonders.

Ingredients:

(Makes twelve pieces)

For the batter:

1 cup plain flour
½ teaspoon instant yeast
1 tablespoon cornstarch
1 tablespoon sugar
¼ teaspoon cardamom powder
1 pinch of salt
1 pinch of saffron
⅓ cup lukewarm milk
lukewarm water as needed, 1/3 cups

For frying and dressing:

oil for deep frying
1/2 cup date syrup
1 tablespoon toasted sesame seeds

Preparation:

Add the flour, yeast, milk, sugar, cornstarch, cardamom powder and saffron into a bowl and mix well.

Slowly add water while gently mixing by hand to get a sticky, almost dough-like batter. Cover with a cloth and allow to rest for 2 hours in a warm place until doubled in size.

Heat oil over medium heat; it should shimmer but not smoke.

Once hot, drop in the batter by the tablespoonful, rolling the dropped balls in the oil with a slotted spoon for even cooking. Fry until deep golden brown in colour, then remove and place on a kitchen towel to drain excess oil.

Arrange in a serving bowl and pour on the date syrup. Finally, sprinkle with sesame seeds.

MINT LEMONADE MOCKTAIL

This frosty drink can be found in every Dubai café in the summer, and for good reason; it's the perfect way to beat the heat.

Ingredients:

6 large ice cubes
1 cup fresh mint leaves, plus sprigs for garnish
2 lemons, juiced, plus slices for garnish
2 teaspoons sugar
1 cup water

Preparation:

Put all the ingredients in a blender and blend until smooth and flecked with green. Pour into glasses and garnish with a slice of lemon and a sprig of mint.

Note:

The addition of rum turns this into an equally refreshing cocktail.

SUMMER SEASON FOOD PLANNING

June till September
Seasonal vegetables and fruits

Aubergine, Beetroot, Broad Beans, Broccoli, Carrots, Cauliflower, Chillies, Zucchini, Cucumber, Potatoes, Radishes, Raspberries, Rocket, Strawberries, Tomatoes, Watercress, Leeks, Lettuce, Peppers, Potatoes, Raspberries, Rocket, Spring Onions, Strawberries, Sweetcorn, Tomatoes, Watercress, White Cabbage, Celery, Kale, Spinach.

Summer Weekly Planner

Week 1	Week 2	Week 3	Week 4

Social Activities and recipe info

Brunches, dinner parties, family get-together, friends staying over

Recipes to try, comments and aide memoire

Shopping List

	Item	Qty
☐		
☐		
☐		
☐		
☐		
☐		
☐		
☐		
☐		
☐		
☐		
☐		
☐		
☐		
☐		
☐		
☐		
☐		
☐		
☐		

Notes

Summer Menu Planner

SUMMER SEASON FOOD PLANNING

June till September
Seasonal vegetables and fruits

Aubergine, Beetroot, Broad Beans, Broccoli, Carrots, Cauliflower, Chillies, Zucchini, Cucumber, Potatoes, Radishes, Raspberries, Rocket, Strawberries, Tomatoes, Watercress, Leeks, Lettuce, Peppers, Potatoes, Raspberries, Rocket, Spring Onions, Strawberries, Sweetcorn, Tomatoes, Watercress, White Cabbage, Celery, Kale, Spinach.

Summer Weekly Planner

Week 1	Week 2	Week 3	Week 4

Social Activities and recipe info

Brunches, dinner parties, family get-together, friends staying over

Recipes to try, comments and aide memoire

Shopping List

Item	Qty

Notes

Summer Menu Planner

TIPS FOR SUSTAINABLE LIVING

I have always loved animals, and first became a vegetarian at the age of twelve when it occurred to me how similar they are to us humans. I have not eaten meat since then, and I remain the lone vegetarian in my family! Looking back, that was the first time I became aware of how our eating habits directly impact our environment.

Reducing waste always felt intuitively right to me, and though I like shopping as much as the next person, excessive consumption never appealed to me. My lifestyle was naturally what might now be called low impact, but I did not actually encounter the term 'sustainability' until 2005. My formal introduction to the subject that would truly transform my life came from Dr. Dirk Matten, one of my MBA professors, and it led me to the career I have now.

Striving to reduce waste on a personal level is of great importance to me, and I try to do so in many little ways every day. One of my priorities is to eliminate food waste in my kitchen, and I would love to help you do so in yours.

The best place to start, of course, is not to buy more than you can eat. To that end, I have included menu planning tools in this book. Sitting down to list meal ideas for the coming days and taking into consideration what ingredients you already have at home before going shopping is a great way to ensure you don't come home with more than you need.

I have also been discovering ways to use food scraps from my kitchen in my garden. For instance, I chop up banana peels and scatter them, mixing them in with the soil. They completely disappear in a few days and nourish your plants. The same can be done with things like crushed eggshells, potato peels, parsley stems or oranges and lemons that have been squeezed, the latter of which also acts as a natural repellent to some pests.

I only buy loose tea and coffee, in part to cut down on extra packaging as well as to avoid teabags, which many people don't know can't be composted because they contain plastic. I then save my coffee grounds and spent tea leaves, let them cool down to room temperature and add a little water. You can use that concoction to water hydrangeas; mine turned stunningly vibrant shades of purple, blue and hot pink. The nutrients contained in tea and coffee also make this mixture excellent to use for rosebushes, helping them to grow many more blooms,

Tips for Sustainable Living

as long as you make sure to deadhead them regularly.

I like to try and plant things from my kitchen, like apple cores and avocado pits. I have had a lot of success so far, except with lemons which refuse to take root! This habit has also led me to discover more things I can reuse; items like paper bags and cardboard tubes can be filled with soil and compost to provide the perfect place for seedlings to sprout indoors. Once they are strong enough to be moved outside, they can be transferred directly into the ground without needing to disturb the roots, as the cardboard and paper will biodegrade and disappear within a few months.

I have successfully used these tips both in the ground and in pots, so they will all still work if you don't have access to a garden.

SANDRA ANANI
FOUNDER AND DIRECTOR
SUSTAINABILITY TO ACTION (STA)

Sandra Anani is a recognised sustainability and governance expert, with over 20 years' experience. She has dedicated her career to sustainable development of business, starting in 1994 with British Airways, where she managed operations and commercial roles. In 2003 Sandra joined the British Airports Authority, covering operations, assurance and policy at BAA.

Sandra joined Abu Dhabi Airports Company to lead the development of corporate sustainability. In 2013 Sandra worked with the Abu Dhabi Sustainability Group to develop sustainability communications and events. Sandra is currently preparing a research proposal in application for her PhD on sustainability and organisational behaviour.

Her diverse career has been complemented by her ongoing commitment to academic development, including an MBA in International Business Management from the University of London and a Master in Laws in Corporate Governance from the University of Law in Bloomsbury, London and is a certified governance professional. Sandra is a member of the Corporate Governance Institute in London.

MENU PLANNING FOR GATHERINGS

Event Name:

Date:

Number of guests:

Names and dietary requirements:

Table decorations

Tablescape, cloth, napkin

Place name cards

Party favours

Flowers

Candles

Prepare and print menu for the table

Other

Nibbles	Starter	Main	Dessert	Cooking Schedule

Drinks

Nibbles:

Starter:

Main:

Dessert:

Post meal:

Comments:

Notes

MENU PLANNING FOR GATHERINGS

Event Name:

Date:	
Number of guests:	
Names and dietary requirements:	

Table decorations
- Tablescape, cloth, napkin
- Place name cards
- Party favours
- Flowers
- Candles
- Prepare and print menu for the table
- Other

Nibbles	Starter	Main	Dessert	Cooking Schedule

Drinks

- Nibbles:
- Starter:
- Main:
- Dessert:
- Post meal:
- Comments:

Notes

MENU PLANNING FOR GATHERINGS

Event Name:

Date:

Number of guests:

Names and dietary requirements:

Table decorations

Tablescape, cloth, napkin

Place name cards

Party favours

Flowers

Candles

Prepare and print menu for the table

Other

Nibbles	Starter	Main	Dessert	Cooking Schedule

Drinks

Nibbles:

Starter:

Main:

Dessert:

Post meal:

Comments:

Notes

MENU PLANNING FOR GATHERINGS

Event Name:

Date:	
Number of guests:	
Names and dietary requirements:	

Table decorations

- Tablescape, cloth, napkin
- Place name cards
- Party favours
- Flowers
- Candles
- Prepare and print menu for the table
- Other

Nibbles	Starter	Main	Dessert	Cooking Schedule

Drinks

Nibbles:

Starter:

Main:

Dessert:

Post meal:

Comments:

Notes

MENU PLANNING FOR GATHERINGS

Event Name:

Date:

Number of guests:

Names and dietary requirements:

Table decorations

Tablescape, cloth, napkin

Place name cards

Party favours

Flowers

Candles

Prepare and print menu for the table

Other

Nibbles	Starter	Main	Dessert	Cooking Schedule

Drinks

Nibbles:

Starter:

Main:

Dessert:

Post meal:

Comments:

Notes

MENU PLANNING FOR GATHERINGS

Event Name:

Date:	
Number of guests:	
Names and dietary requirements:	

Table decorations
- Tablescape, cloth, napkin
- Place name cards
- Party favours
- Flowers
- Candles
- Prepare and print menu for the table
- Other

Nibbles	Starter	Main	Dessert	Cooking Schedule

Drinks
- Nibbles:
- Starter:
- Main:
- Dessert:
- Post meal:
- Comments:

Notes

MENU PLANNING FOR GATHERINGS

Event Name:

Date:	
Number of guests:	
Names and dietary requirements:	

Table decorations

- Tablescape, cloth, napkin
- Place name cards
- Party favours
- Flowers
- Candles
- Prepare and print menu for the table
- Other

Nibbles	Starter	Main	Dessert	Cooking Schedule

Drinks

- Nibbles:
- Starter:
- Main:
- Dessert:
- Post meal:
- Comments:

Notes

MENU PLANNING FOR GATHERINGS

Event Name:

Date:	
Number of guests:	
Names and dietary requirements:	

Table decorations

- Tablescape, cloth, napkin
- Place name cards
- Party favours
- Flowers
- Candles
- Prepare and print menu for the table
- Other

Nibbles	Starter	Main	Dessert	Cooking Schedule

Drinks

- Nibbles:
- Starter:
- Main:
- Dessert:
- Post meal:
- Comments:

Notes

MENU PLANNING FOR GATHERINGS

Event Name:

Date:	
Number of guests:	
Names and dietary requirements:	

Table decorations

- Tablescape, cloth, napkin
- Place name cards
- Party favours
- Flowers
- Candles
- Prepare and print menu for the table
- Other

Nibbles	Starter	Main	Dessert	Cooking Schedule

Drinks

- Nibbles:
- Starter:
- Main:
- Dessert:
- Post meal:
- Comments:

Notes

MENU PLANNING FOR GATHERINGS

Event Name:

Date:

Number of guests:

Names and dietary requirements:

Table decorations

Tablescape, cloth, napkin

Place name cards

Party favours

Flowers

Candles

Prepare and print menu for the table

Other

Nibbles | Starter | Main | Dessert | Cooking Schedule

Drinks

Nibbles:

Starter:

Main:

Dessert:

Post meal:

Comments:

Notes

www.ingramcontent.com/pod-product-compliance
Lightning Source LLC
Chambersburg PA
CBRC090903080526
44587CB00009B/181